DEDICATION

To Mike Foster, who taught me boredom is a choice and the only failure is one of imagination. To my mother who taught me that strangeness is a thing to be fascinated by. To Alan Watts, who's humor and radiant mind has inspired generations.

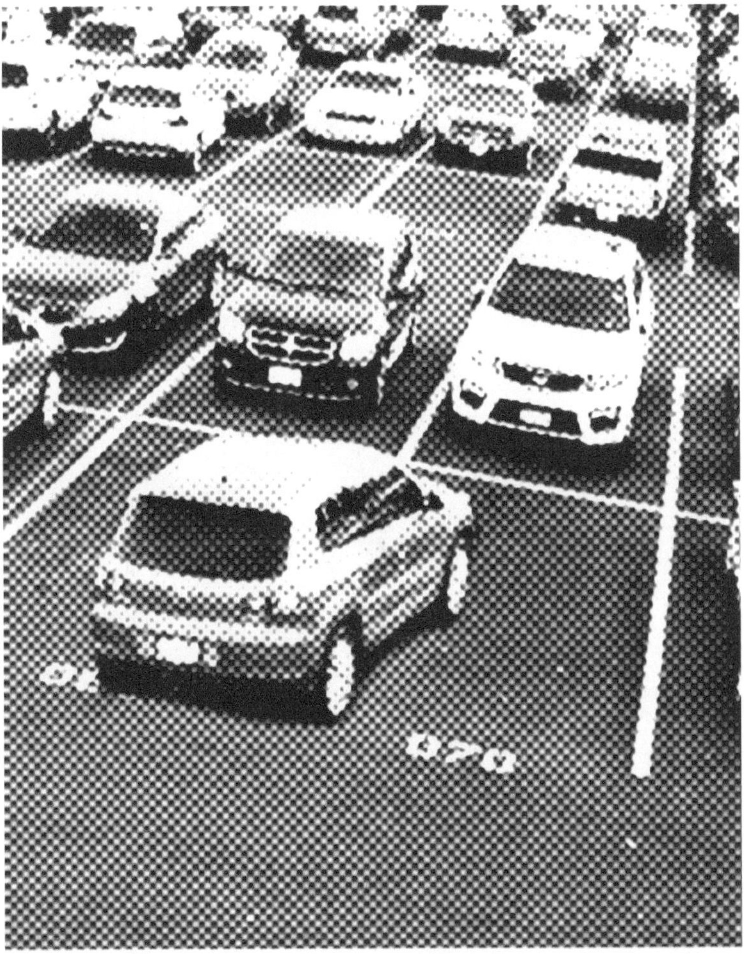

An Exquisite Failure
Unexpected lessons from art and life

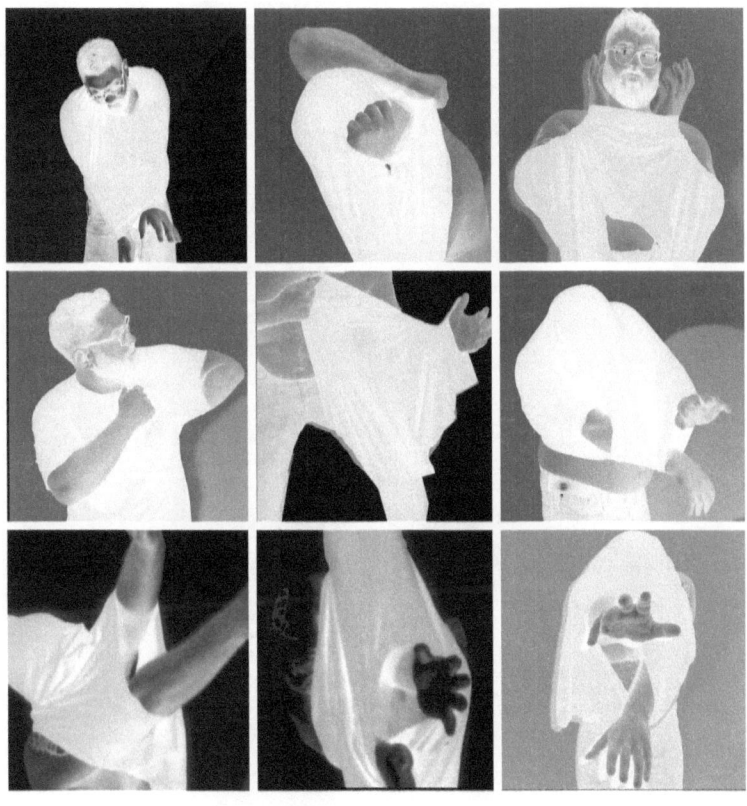

Reza Ghanad

Copyright © 2017 Reza Ghanad

All rights reserved.

ISBN-10: 1976320445
ISBN-13: 978-1976320446

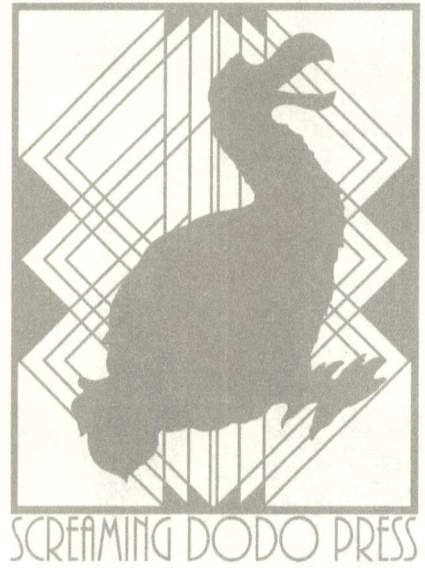

CONTENTS

Introduction

The rules of failure

One and the same, a love story

I'm addicted to myself

Why does this always happen to me?

How to fall effectively

The wrong numbers

Making bad drawings

Failure to finish

About the author

ACKNOWLEDGMENTS

Thanks to Amanda for being my editor and my best friend.

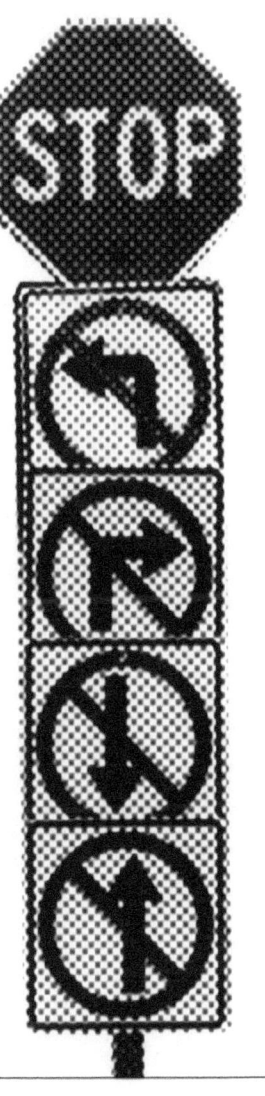

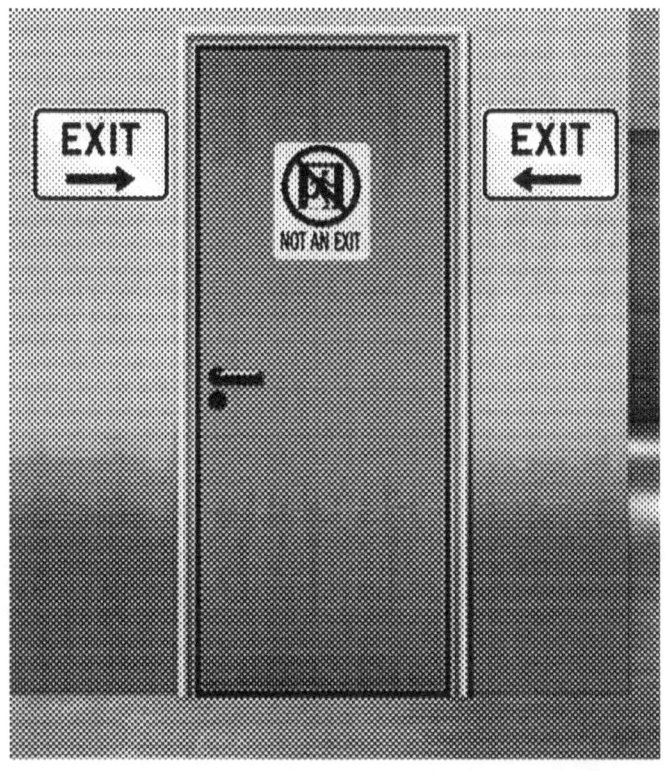

INTRODUCTION

We live in a time when many things are in a state of failure. Our economic models have failed, our social contracts have failed, and our educational systems are failing. The very ideals of American democracy are failing. Those of you from other parts of the world you may fill in whatever failure is happening in your land, as rest assured there are many. I would like to suggest that all great things are developed from a series of failures. As Darwin points out it's not that nature is attempting to reach a kind of perfection, it's rather the organisms that best adapt to failure that go on to thrive. Adapting and learning from failure is the mark of a successful life.

A serious and good philosophical work could be written consisting entirely of jokes.

Ludwig Wittgenstein

I would go further and suggest that a good life could be lived consisting entirely of blunders. Failure is a thing we are all intimately familiar with. As an artist, failure is the most common phenomena in my process. Trial and error is a great method for improving methods and learning the nature of any subject. Unfortunately, it doesn't make the emotional effects any easier to take. This book endeavors to illuminate the concept of failure through visual art and story telling. The purpose of which is to make better art, and a better life through the utilization of failure.

Where do I begin to tell you of my numerous failures? The time I asked a girl, that had no interest in me, to the "sock hop" when I was seven years old? There's my stuttering, emotional, attempt to speak for my PAFA class at graduation. It's memory continues to make me cringe. My speech, of course, had to follow THEE Sir Howard Hodgkins' booming, godlike voice. He's a knight for f#*k sake!

Or, should I start with the hundreds of failed sketches and studies I have painted? I discovered that it was not the individual paintings that mattered it was the journey from one failure to another that propelled the work forward. There is no overall failure in art, there is only unfortunate bits of the journey. These sentiments can often be so cliched that it's nearly impossible to add anything new. I think of the inspirational jpg's or earnest Instagram posts of the world. I considered this, when I began to write this book, and worried that the reader would just pass it up as yet another artist's puffed up nonsense. Not to mention I'm clearly no celebrity or famous athlete, so why listen to me? I considered this while taking in the fact I haven't sold a single copy of my first book, Thoughts on Self. A book on mindfulness; which is a trait, I have very little of. I think about this while processing the fact that not only will I most probably die in complete obscurity, and that I've carefully created material for an entire generation of "Trolls". So if we are to believe the thought that failure breeds success, then I should be on my way to the championship now!

AN EXQUISITE FAILURE

I have not failed. I've just found 10,000 ways that won't work.

Thomas A. Edison

    Failure has become as ubiquitous as light-bulbs for me. There is a sort of dark humor in my numerous failures. The way that all the little elements align to make the most irritating of all possible outcomes has made me a believer in a divine comedian. As if one is the main character in a sitcom about a guy who just cant get a break. One of the reasons I can't handle "cringe comedy" shows, is that I relate too much to the poor schlump making all the bad decisions. In short, famous or not, I'm an expert on losing. This book will be my living testimony to my extraordinary talents in this field. I can say with certainty I am "writing what I know".

    As for you dear reader, I hope to make the ride at least interesting for you, the way that one can't look away from a car crash, or that strange pleasure we get while watching epic wipe outs. "Face first into a cake", should be the name of my biography. This is sure to be one of the greatest artistic failures I've ever achieved. I hope to wow you with how perfectly horrible it will be! Seriously though, failure works as a powerful catalyst in the artist process. But in all seriousness, I will try to show you it can help you in life, even though that seems a contradiction in terms. Oh! There will be some neat pictures too.

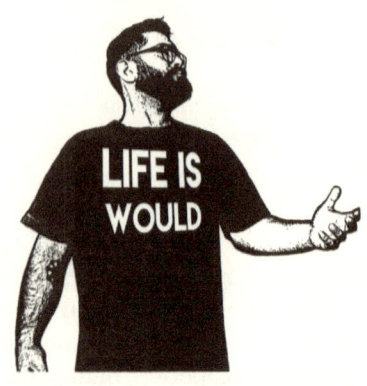

THE RULES OF FAILURE

<u>Rule one:</u> **thou shall not make a self-referential work of art. Said work will most certainly contain circular logic, and will suffer from a lack of consistent structure.**

To facilitate this process of discovering failure's ability to aid in the art process, I'm going to use <u>this very book</u> as a conceptual work of art on the subject. From here on out, I will use the subject as an artistic element, and not, instead attempt to elaborate on a philosophical or cultural ramifications of the idea, with any semblance of scientific authority. **Starting now**, everything is a conceptual piece or "artwork" and not a book about failure. From this point forward you are watching an object lesson in failure unfold. A self-referential analysis of failure as failure. I already broke the first rule..

<u>Rule two:</u> **thou shall not make up arbitrary rules in the style of the ten commandments or any other historical document. It will beg comparison, and doom the ideas which one is trying to convey.**

One of the biggest mistakes visual artists make when they go to art school is that they confuse the experience of getting educated for the artistic process. Part of the reason Postmodernism even happened was that Modernism made the elements of painting, for example, part of the subject of the work of art. The fundamentals of a paintings' structure where laid bare, as a subject to be pondered. Finally culminating in Minimalism which emphasized the "thingness" of things. Soon this was followed by the perspective of, making pictures about the history, and development of formalities of image making. Hence, "self-referential". One could argue quite easily that art has always been self-referential, in some manner or other. The difference now is that, art being self-reflective, is a subject of art.

Those who don't wonder about the contingency of the world's existence are mentally deficient.

Arthur Schopenhauer

Rule three: **thou shall not edify one's own ideas by quoting smarter people, or make historical references, one cannot speak on with verifiable authority.**

Already botched that one..

Rule four: **thou shall not make sudden changes in format for seemingly no reason. Especially, then emphasize the moment, by highlighting the change. Unless it is of consequence to the narrative. Which it certainly is not in this case.**

As long as the structure and context are understood, or at the very least consistent, the viewer will eventually "get it". Furthermore, academics will carefully elucidate all the tentative (possibly fictional) conceptual links with other works of art that have been given institutional approval. This effort to create a logical "grand narrative" has come under question more recently though, and has been slowly eroding in the face of Feminism and a new internationalism. Minority or non-mainstream perspectives, new identity sub-cultures, and non-western aesthetics have begun to make the landscape of art making so complex that the only thing keeping any coherent notion of an "art world" is capital. Not surprisingly, this is unfolding in the milieu of the most critical anti-colonialist and anti-materialist art theory ever. At least theoretically.

Capital seems to be the only determinant of value in today's global art "economy". Unfortunately, capital has some built in problems such as: hegemony, institutional greed, academically veiled self-interest, and strategic market manipulation. So artists are tackling these failing hierarchies as material for their projects. Some alternatively have made themselves shining beacons of glossy materialism as a response. Those artists are gross, don't feed them. Everyone will be better off when those artists are seen as a sad outmoded representation, of a sad outmoded lifestyle.

Rule five: thou shall not present your opinions as facts regarding systems too vast for one to have a comprehensive overview of.

One of the most ambiguous elements of system failure in art making, I believe, is the prevalence of action as art. What I mean is social engagement works for example, that are indistinguishable from, "just being a person in the world doing stuff". Another might be, performance pieces that resemble everyday situations, unadulterated by any clear demarcation from a mundane act. When the line between the conscious making of a "work of art" and the act of simply "being" is evaporated, you end up right where you started. If anything can be art, than everything is art, and therefore any form of being alive is making art. Which is fine, but why then privilege the title at all? This logical concludes that the discussion of "what art is" is apparently of no consequence. I'm left feeling as though art has fallen into that hole of, "it is what it is". Furthermore, this then raises the question: if understanding the

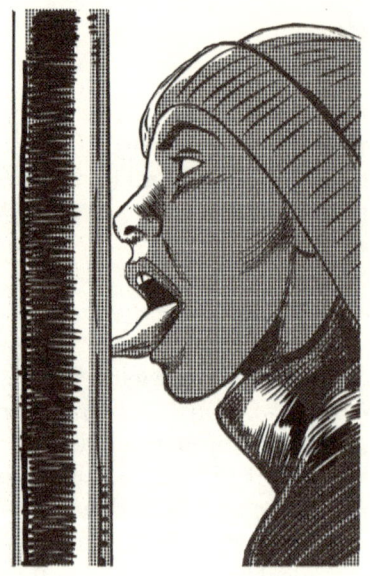

nature of art is not the purpose of art, what is it instead? I would suggest, you and I have just done that.

Rule six: thou shall not use an inherently problematic language to describe it's own failings. One of the problems with attempting to make a "true" or "honest" work of art is that the maker of the art is in the worst position to be objective or honest. This is because of the simple reason that no one is objective, when their effort is on the line. No one is looking to dissect their artistic creations, looking to poke holes in it, just for fun. Our minds are biologically designed to edit out the bits of reality that are not necessary for biological survival, and the bits that threaten our very fragile ego image most of all. In addition, there are countless programs of control, that were designed before we where born, that effect any objectivity regarding ourselves, and our place in our society. The complex power struggles of the ruling classes have been a PR battle for the minds of the public since Edward Bernays[1]. These establishments are designed to keep us from discovering systemic corruption, the manipulation of our thoughts, and labor. One could argue before the use of propaganda science, the church had already invented the ultimate form of self regulated mind control. The subconscious shields our illusion of agency from ever really seeing our fragility. The powerful impact our circumstances have on our lives is whitewashed in order to maintain the narrative of free will. Unfiltered awareness can lead to depression and sometimes riots. In short, there is more evidence pointing in the direction of our collective delusions and misrepresentations, regarding reality, than the presence of concrete "truth". This idea is extremely upsetting. Artists want to believe they have a direct contact with the pulse of existence.

The perfect failure is: to know you are likely wrong, corrupt, ill prepared, or irrelevant, and continue to make art as if it's important. You passionately continue undeterred as there is no doubt, that every mark is significant. Another way to put this might be, "being willfully ignorant that you're being willfully ignorant". About the physical realities of ones art, and the life this path will most likely dump on your lap.

Allen Watts once pondered, if you were capable of dreaming

---

1   Austrian-American theorist in the field of public relations and propaganda, referred to as "the father of public relations".

anything you wanted each night, you'd probably dream up a kind of heaven for yourself filled with all the things that you most want. But eventually you'd tire of this and realize adventures are only fun if there is risk, or something at stake. Watt's then suggests that God decided to forget he's God, and be a person that has no idea that they are the divine incarnate. He suggests that we are all part of the great cosmic play, and are coming to realize we are in fact the ultimate divine presence (that has willfully forgotten itself for fun). The thing is, do YOU think your God? I don't really feel like I am. Many artists might be prone to occasionally acting like they are. As for me, if I am a god just pretending to be a broke artist.. well heck, I think I've had enough of that. Let's try being stupendously successful for a while!

Another interpretation maybe that life is like a dream in which one starts out a baby and ends up being a parent of another being. One sees the process happen all over again from an increasingly advantaged perspective. Teaching the next generation may have been the process our god myth arose from. As if we were, in away, "waking up" to the potential abilities and knowledge humanity is capable of, through the act of raising ourselves. and then our children.

A thinker sees his own actions as experiments and questions.. as attempts to find out something. Success and failure are for him answers above all.

Friedrich Nietzsche

<u>Rule seven:</u> Art should be revelatory, even if only of one's personality flaws.

I would love to tell you that there is an academically sound point to all of this. The loose connections and tentative theories is a part of the perpetual hamster wheel of being an artist. Oddly, I have written several pages of text in this process of failing to make cogent ideas. We return full circle to rule one stating this would not be self-referential. It appears failure to follow the rules has resulted in writing this book. It appears that even failing at art is making art. Now you can understand why Giacometti, Morandi, or Lucien Freud could spend a lifetime painting the same damn subject over and over. They never quite felt like they nailed it. **The process of discovering an artistic truth is like rehearsing for a speech you lost the notes for.** Ultimately, artists just struggle to come back to the same place they originated, the search for meaning. They already have won the war, but continue pretending for themselves that the battle had just begun. We are always, in fact, talking to an echo – having a circular argument, in a way. This futility has the wonderful side effect of leaving lots of art for us to enjoy. For the artists this appears seemingly the opposite of progress. The various attempts to express an idea an artist produces is a record of their failures. Failure is the black hole from which all art emerges. Despite all our fears that it's impossible or a lost cause, the "light" of creation flows out of the black hole's inescapable gravity. The "failure" of the universe to be a perfect symmetrical machine is reflected in our own oddness and asymmetry. It's is this flawed technical execution (or dither) that saves us from a lifeless universe. It seems failure is necessary for life to exist, for people to become stronger, and for art to happen.

Sometimes one person's disaster is another person's liberation. For example, the freedom of choice that the birth control pill gave women. It was the single most powerful transformation for the quality of women's lives. Reproductive rights is still one of the most controversial topics in America. It takes a generation to realize the benefits of a revolutionary technology. It seems in this case about 19 to 20 years, basically between availability and understanding. For example, the birth control pill was made available 1960. Then in 1965 the pill was made legal for married couples. Nineteen years latter (a period of time similar to the time it takes for a child to be born and then graduate from US high school) the words "Feminist" and "Enlightenment" where used in equal measure (see figure a). People need to live out the consequences of their actions to contribute their wisdom to their next generation. No one can understand their choices until after they have made them. I interpret this data as a generation of women telling their daughters about the benefits of staying single and/or not having children right away (or ever), due to their experience having done otherwise. As well as the value of feminist perspective emerging form the new options some had taken advantage of.

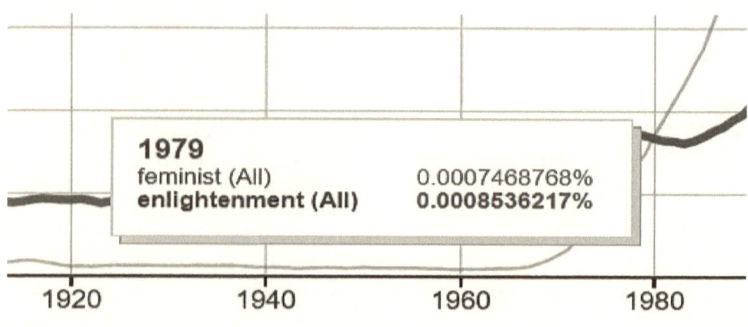

Figure A

Rates of education for women reflect this transformation as well. In 1960, when the pill was first available, 54% of men went to college and 37.9% of women went to college. By 1980 men where at 46.7% and women now surpassed in enrollment at 51.8%. All birth rate markers have steadily declined ever since. The number of women that had management roles increased from 15% in 1960 to around 36% by the eighties. The biggest jump occurred between the 70's and the 90's (Sources: N.C.E.S., and The Census Bureau). I conclude that in the time that passed mothers realized the benefits and taught their daughters to make their own choices. What is a catastrophe in the eyes of Evangelicals, has become a blessing to women who sought education and financial independence.

There are also other trends of word use, that make for interesting overlaps (found via Google's Ngram viewer). In the effort to justify this premise I'm including events that may show possible motivators. There's always a hint of something failing or malfunctioning in the background of amazing insights. In 1979 the words "failure" and "truth" are used together in equal amounts, and again in 1990. Here are events that occurred in 1979 followed by events that occurred during 1990. Do these events relate to failure and truth?

AN EXQUISITE FAILURE

1979

The State of Ohio pays $675,000 to families of the Kent State shootings victims.

Three Mile Island explosion.

Riot in San Francisco after the verdict for Dan White, assassin of Supervisor Harvey Milk.

The US energy crisis.

The top 4 movies that year:

1. Flatliners

2. Goodfellas

3. The Handmaid's Tale

4. Misery

1990

Financier Michael Milken is sentenced to 10 years in prison, and a fine of $600.

The trial of the skipper of the Exxon Valdez begins.

D.C. Mayor Marion Barry is arrested for drug possession.

The United States enters the recession.

The top 4 movies that year:

1. Alien

2. Apocalypse Now

3. Caligula

4. The Warriors

Source: Wikipedia

I see a failure of the state to protect citizens from corruption, unprecedented environmental disasters, and a failure of our system to tackle economic crisis. The films seem to indicate fear of alien dangers, a dystopian future, rampant criminality, and being at the whim of the unknowable. There's a ten year gap in between these dates that contain the boom and bust of the 80's. The peak was 83, when Scarface was in theaters (lots of coke going around in those days). Psychologically we went on a roller coaster. There was such optimism in the eighties due to the bump in economic growth, and then it came crashing down in a hype hang over.

Rule eight: thou shall not evade the obvious facts, for ones you're more comfortable with.

It would be great to pretend that the world is filled with enlightened beings, attempting to be more aware of what they are doing and why. But let's admit it, most of us are still so selfish and infantile, that they can barely make it through a day without acting like a spoiled five year old. I am doing this daily; and if you think you are not, I wouldn't trust your opinion of yourself. Failure is part of being human. Trying to predict the future and it's consequences is like trying to stop bleeding, with faith. But I can say that the way we are heading looks like a collision course with our collective hubris. The world is so far behind being sustainable, as far as human behavior is concerned, you wouldn't be blamed for wanting all of this to come to a fiery end.

Through accepting failure, instead of blaming others, we stand a chance of improving. Maybe you think our moral compass has gone wrong, or you think we've become more progressive than ever. It does not matter your politics, when you look at facts, everything is failing. We of course need a democratically agreed upon road map, of what success means in order to change that. If we are willing to learn from our blunders, by learning from experience and having the humility to change positions, we just might survive!

(see the failure to observe)

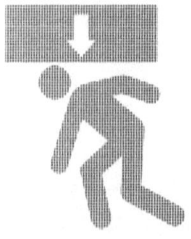

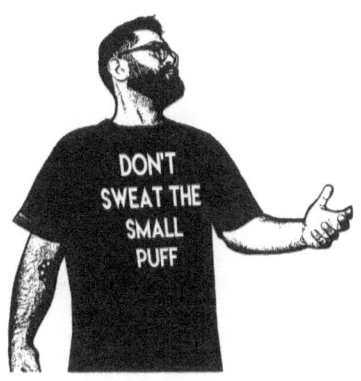

ONE AND THE SAME, A LOVE STORY

In order to love something you must first desire it. Later, you become enamored with it's otherness. Then you become familiar with it and expect it, and have some comfort in it's predictability. Finally you suspect you know it too well. Soon you begin to see it's faults. Which begins to develop into a kind of disdain. "Why can't it be more the way I'd rather it was", you say secretly to yourself. Inevitably, you begin to hate the object of your "love". You begin to be cruel and dismissive of this familiar and flawed thing. Soon, it starts to confirm all of your worst suspicions, and you soon hate the thing you thought you loved so much. This process could be applied to a job, a group of friends, or even a performer.

Why does this happen? Now obviously this doesn't happen as a rule, but this dynamic is so common it's the stuff of soap operas. Why does the honeymoon period end? Why do we know this a thing that happens? Why are the few happy couples so comfortable talking with their loved ones with such easy bluntness? It's extraordinary to meet couples that can work so well together? Why is it so many people are prone to fighting with the ones closest to them with such fierceness? Why are so many suffering in silence, and not communicating with each other their inner self and longing to love and be loved? Because it's difficult, and filled with false steps, and failures along the way.

"Intimate partner violence" is a public health crisis in this country. Estimated to cost the public upwards of $8 billion annually. It is bracing to see the harm in black and white. We harm each other with such commonness that it is a matter of public record. Failure at love is so much a part of our lives that it supports multiple economies. Tinder, Ashley Madison, Dear Abby, Savage Love, Dr. Ruth, and Dr. Phil all owe their fortunes to the failure of people loving properly and/or being loved properly. What does it mean to love properly? Why do we fail at loving each other? I have a feeling it has to do with this questionable idea that we are separate, that we are individuals. The concept of one being physically and mentally separate from the universe you live in is a fallacy. It's an odd thought to digest, but you are in fact inseparable to the air and the space around you – all of this is one "thing". The tragedy of selfishness is that it harms us, going in both directions. 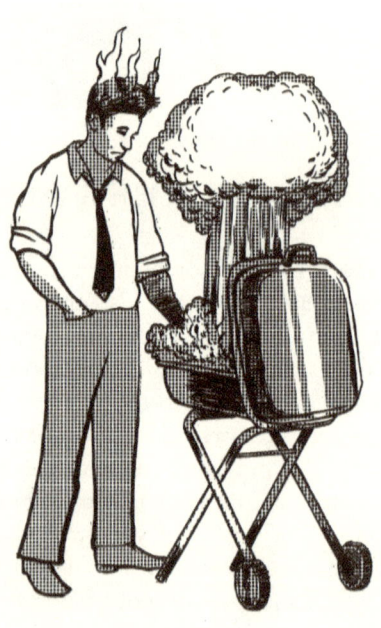 If only we could be truly "objectively selfish", then we might see that what's good for you is exactly the same thing as what's good for the other. The foundation of good dialog is accepting that you are not perfect, and neither are they. We must try every day to not hurt each other.

I didn't fail the test, I just found 100 ways to do it wrong.

Benjamin Franklin

Have you ever noticed how much the highway/road system in the US resembles veins and arteries in a human body? We even use terms like arterial road, or main artery when describing certain roads. For example, a highway is designed to be big and have slow curves, like a main artery, in order to facilitate large numbers of cars/blood cells. Then as we pass into more localized areas the roads slow in speed, and increase in the pitch and frequency of curves. Then finally, the roads become very specific, and the flow is almost crawling. When a road doesn't resemble this body-like logic, car accidents increase and traffic jams occur. This is like a stroke, or blood clot, and then system fails to work properly.

It's as if we are intentionally ignoring how much our own bodies and biology resemble the world that we have been given and have constructed. As if, there is some fear that if we accept ourselves as a semi-predictable organism, that functions in a larger and more generalized pattern, it will lessen our value as sentient beings. When corporations attempt to record our purchasing habits and behaviors (Pharmacy membership cards, grocery coupon cards, Google searches) we bristle at the thought of our mundane actions being recorded. Why? I wager, because it makes us feel small, and a thing that can be explained easily. We complain about privacy. Have you ever considered why do you care if someone knows about your trivial purchases of gum and toilet paper? No one likes to be categorized or explained in terms that resemble a weather report (Yet, if you are as old as I am, you will remember that weather prediction went from being almost completely unreliable, to pretty damn good). Of course if we keep destroying the ecosystem, the only thing predictable about the weather will be it sucks. We treat the world as separate, so we don't see that the failure of the environment, is a failure in ourselves. Knowing ourselves is knowing the world.

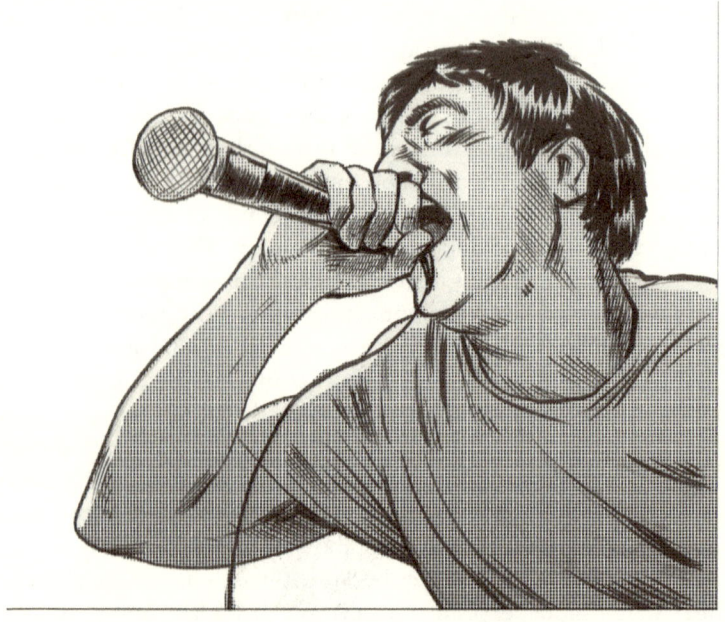

So now I return to the subject of failing at love. How does this concept of body/mental egotism relate? When we believe that we are separate from the elements in our environment, or other organisms, it makes it easy for us to act like a selfish jerk without guilt. Remind yourself how easy it was, as a teenager, to make fun of the kids that where part of a different group than you. Think about how easily some can condemn a, so called, "race" as a whole. As if a skin color implies behavior. As if race isn't an arbitrary label invented in order to separate us even further. Such as it is for gender, and political opinion. We choose to believe in separation because it suits our fragile sense of worth. If we think that we are unworthy of praise and benefits, we begin to "fight or flight". **Most people fear being irrelevant more than anything**. Why, if we are in fact so awesome, do we fear being perceived as lesser? Why do we become violent when we think another group or person is rising above us in importance? Because our reptile brain still thinks we are fighting for fruit on the savanna. I'm not sure, but maybe we just have a culturally programmed obsession with competition?

 Why do we fail at love? Possibly because the only person that some can care about is themselves. That is the ugliest truth that no one wants to admit – initially. Our ego is the seat of the idea of separateness. The newly formed sense-of-self drove our primitive ancestors to survive a hostile world, the way that self interest is supposedly pushing DNA, or free market Capitalism. But maybe that strategy has seen it's day and should be left behind with the A-track.

I choose to believe that our universe endeavors to make our failures into gold, the gold of being truly and fully aware. This is in order to inspire a fully aware person, not just a survivor of the "rat race". A person that can achieve great things, because you can adapt to failure, and learn from your mistakes. Because you can see that everyone is you, in different clothes. To finally see the unavoidable truth that we humans are alone in this universe, with each other. Maybe I'm wrong, but if an extraterrestrial advanced species exists, they won't talk to us until we can at least get along with each other. Also, if there is a divine designer it appears we were left with the car keys and no road map. So let us consider how can we do better, even if it's just for fun in an art book. I'll defer to a wiser soul than myself, Thich Nhat Hanh. He asks us to understand that when others harm you, it is because they are suffering in some way, it is rarely originated in the intention to harm you.

The failure to love, or to be loved properly, can evolve and develop you. Sometimes in a negative way, and if your lucky, in a positive way. When I got divorced, it was the culmination of so many wrong turns for all concerned. We did not understand each other because we where not really capable of it. We did not take the time to really say what needed to be said. We didn't communicate with each other successfully, because we did not have the words to express our feelings at the time. We didn't know it was, OK not to be OK so were we terrible people? Were we people who where unprepared for that challenge? How can you understand someone else, when you don't even know what you're doing and why? Our thoughts and actions are the result of personal pain **and** joy, and we must get to know what makes us feel either carefully. We learn how to make someone else happy by experiencing happiness ourselves, otherwise you would lack the imagination to please others. You must love yourself before you can love someone else, duh. Self-confidence is respecting your value, and potential, and is good practice for respecting others. The evidence is in the results.

> *We are all failures- at least the best of us are.*
>
> *J.M. Barrie*

Ask a recovering addict how they fought their disease. I'll bet they will say, they are realized that they were hurting themselves, and they had to learn to love themselves more carefully. Then, they will remind you that it helps to love others in turn. Maybe you have seen how others suffer with addiction. Addiction comes in so many different shapes. Always remember, everyone is addicted to something. We are addicted to love, and we are addicted to the mental traps that can stop love from thriving.

- According to the National Survey on Drug Use and Health, 21.5 million American adults had substance abuse problems in 2014.

- Jacqueline Howard of CNN is quoted saying in 2016, "The average American spends nearly half a day staring at a screen". This was based on Neilson ratings information.

(see a failure to be compassionate)

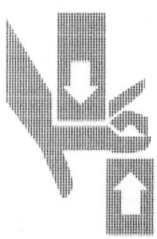

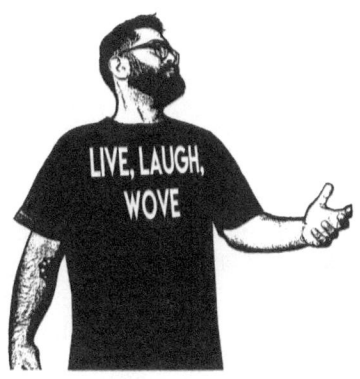

I'M ADDICTED TO MYSELF

What does it mean to be addicted to yourself? It's a strange sentiment or concept. Addiction is a need for something desired, that must be satiated or there's hell to pay. What does it look like to be addicted to one's self? How can one be addicted to that which is seemingly always present? Let us consider other addictions that are omnipresent:

Everyone is addicted to the idea of having a destiny..

to the idea that if we "don't do this", or if "we do that", it will improve our situation..

to, the idea that other people are a threat in one way or another,

and to the idea that they are objective about what is happening to them.

If you don't feel that this is true for you, congratulations, you're in recovery! Wouldn't it be great if we could have an instruction manual on the subject of human suffering? A text that hasn't been altered by politicians, businessman, lawyers, popes, priests, and every other interested party – that had some insight about what we are doing here. Why is it that the discussion of life's meaning always comes with an application to one club or another?

Why can't the nature of existence be a matter of public discourse, and therefore a topic of interest equal to the weather, or a sports outcome? Why are we waiting for someone to write that book for us, when we could be living it now? Because it hurts? Because becoming more real is uncomfortable? Is it too much work?

Trying to be aware is a full time job, above and beyond, all the other jobs you have. One must be an employee, a citizen, a mother, a father, a boss, a dreamer, a (name anything).. AND always pushing the envelope of consciousness. It's unfair, and it's annoying! Even our prophets and sages eventually become another form of addiction to the self: "I'm a Buddhist, I'm Muslim, I'm a Scientologist", these are all titles you place on yourself like decoration. These words only "mean something" when you fill them with your heart. These traditions are only as good as what you put into this process of developing as a person.

So we are left now with addiction to self, as a very tough nut to crack indeed. I would like to present you with a free form self analysis:

"I think that I am a person with a name, and I'm pretty sure that I exist, and other people around me also exist, and are not me. I also, hold opinions that I got from other people, that I assume are correct. I rarely have opportunity to test the opinions of people more powerful/important than me, and I cannot be sure my thoughts are objective for this reason, among others. My senses make me sure that a world exists outside of me, even if I'm not present to perceive it. I learn things about the world when I look carefully at it, but I can't be sure that what I've learned is the whole story. I can't be sure that my information will lead to an understanding of reality".

AN EXQUISITE FAILURE

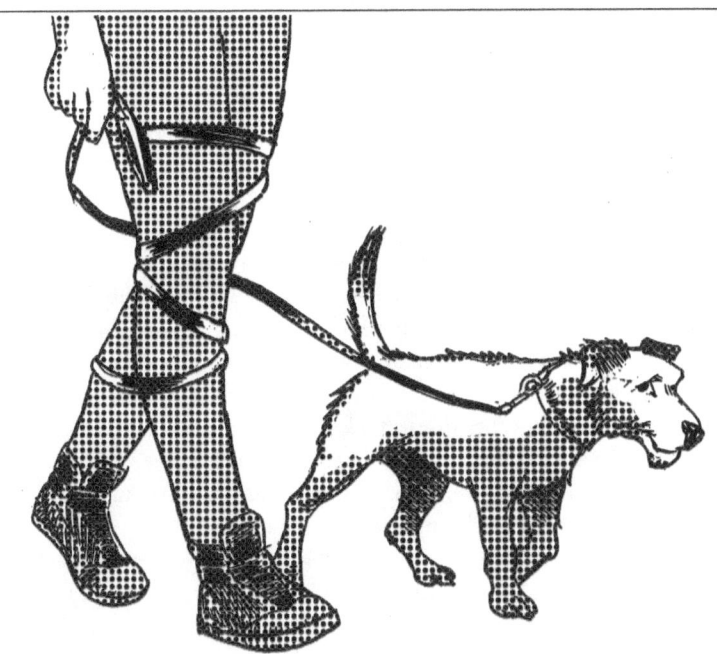

Can we be sure sure that this (reality) is in fact happening, in the way that we perceive it to be? I'm sure that I'm not sure. Can you be so certain, if you have to pull only from what you've personally experienced, first hand? I don't believe you can convincingly. Before I sound as though I am making a case for Solipsism[2], I would offer a psychoanalytic take on this theory. Image our addiction to self, is in fact a fear. The fear that the story we've been told (or we tell ourselves) is inaccurate. The stories we are told, are told by people. You are a person.. are you absolutely positive that you are always seeing clearly? All I have to do is miss a meal and I become nearly insane. What do you suppose the world looks like when you have no preconceptions, and are left only with raw reality (read up on DMT)? This is a real dilemma; how can we be objective about our own perceptions, when we are already running on so many borrowed ideas? We tend to address these

---

2   Solipsism argues that knowledge of anything outside one's own mind is uncertain. The outer world and other minds cannot be known and might not exist outside the imagination. This position can go further to the conclude that the world and other minds do not exist.

abstract questions by deferring to some process of majority opinion or through faith. For some it comes in the form of science, alternatively some rely on mythologies.

But ideology is a seductive trap. It offers easy answers with just enough pain to seem legitimate. There's this big club, and it has benefits, and a lot of support systems. It seems awfully superior to winging it on your own, and possibly being called a cracked pot. But ultimately ideology is an addiction to canned solutions. Addiction to an ideology is worse than addiction to drugs. Drugs will eventually kill you, when used in excess. Faith will consume your mind forever, neutralizing any adaptive thinking that may threaten the fragile sense of holy superiority. It puts you on a celestial pedestal. Who doesn't like being told they are the most important thing in the universe, and for some the scum of the earth? Not only does delusion come in the form of narcissism, it has ways of satisfying the masochist as well. Furthermore, ideology can be like a parasitical virus when it encounters a receptive ego/mind. It is uniquely suited to use your minds structure, and desires, to keep you captive (like any screen). It's as if an idea can be a virus, and has an ability to kill the host in order to maintain it's continued existence. Let us consider how ideological delusion systems resemble the qualities and attributes of deadly infectious disease:

Infectivity: delusion enters the mind of a person, multiplies it's hold in the consciousness, and makes the person self identify as a "follower". The victim becomes hooked, and it becomes the frame of everything in their life.

Pathogenicity: idealogy has very specific mental effects on the host. Such as euphoria, delusions of grandeur, hallucinations, self-immolation, and a tendency towards restricted thought patterns. Defensiveness and paranoia develop into psychopathic outcomes.

Virulence: The profound destructive power of faith is recorded over and over in human history: The Crusades, the Inquisition, The German Peasants' War, The Eighty Years' War, the Huguenot Wars, The Thirty Years' War, Northern Ireland, 9/11, and ISIS to name a few examples.

Toxigenicity: Violence, sexism, and bigotry abounds when mythology is coupled with political power.

Resistance: Modern medical advancements, and scientific inquiry into every aspect of our universe has pointed invariable to no known mysticism being absolutely correct (or even a little correct for that matter). superstition has not contributed to any useful understanding of our universe in regards to health, physics, or advancement in any form of technology. Yet most of humanity (89%) holds to their contradicting delusion systems while enjoying the benefits of scientific discovery. This perpetuates ongoing hostilities and under-appreciates sciences' contribution to everything we do.

Antigenicity: As education increases, and modern advances become more available, most people begin to take traditional spirituality less seriously. The more secular the society, the more humane and free it becomes.

In other words, the more successful the society, the less superstitious it is. Also, interestingly, the more secular the society the lower the crime rate. The United Nations' 2011 Global Study on Homicide found that in the ten nations with the highest homicide rates, the population was consistently overwhelmingly religious. Colombia, Mexico, El Salvador and Brazil are the most theistic nations in the world and have the highest rates of homicide. The nations with the lowest homicide rates are very secular. Of these, the least faith driven nations such as Sweden, Japan, Norway and the Netherlands had the lowest of all rates of homicide. Ideology may not be the number one reason for war on earth, but it appears that it has a powerful and unambiguous correlation with violence. Another amazing statistical revelation is that there is a direct correlation between unwanted pregnancies and an increase of crime. Steven Levitt, author of "Freakonomics", found that as states legalized abortion, crime took a notable dip. His findings concluded that as young women had children, often too young to financially cope with the burden, they struggled to parent successfully. Often, left to raise the child with very little help, or resources. This made spending time with that child more difficult due to, often low paying jobs, with long hours. This often meant the child was raised in a lower income area, which increased exposure to drugs and criminal behavior. Children who are not actively parented, through fault or not, often become delinquent. This is an experience I can speak to personally. As a young person my mother had to raise my sister and I on her own. This put the burden of making an income and maintaining a household on her alone. We lived in a rougher school district and my grades dipped. I became depressed and distant. My mother sensed the negative trend and moved us to a quieter community with better schools. We may have lived in the projects, but my education brought me up. I graduated with an A average, and was in more than one honors class. I am certain this was because of my environment. Poverty is the single most powerful factor to the development of a successful mind. Countless studies have pointed to this, yet there are still idiots quoting the "Bell Curve".

Righteousness and xenophobia are very dangerous, it blinds us to our shared humanity. I would suggest that an addiction to an ideology is like being sick with a very infectious and deadly virus. It's only cure is a good education and science. What does it mean to be educated to me? I do not believe that there is only one

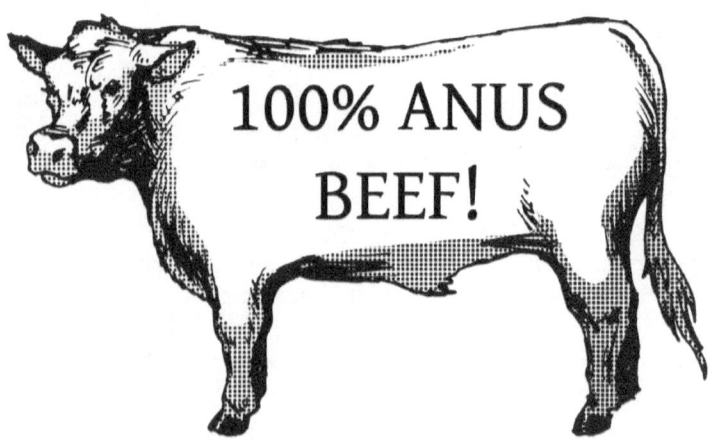

determination of a good education. The characteristics I'm referring to are: critical thinking skills, being considerate of direct experience in determining the nature of phenomena, a sensitivity to cultural differences and contexts, an understanding of the need to suspend judgments before study, and a healthy sense of skepticism (among other things). These are attributes that where instilled in my home and supported by excellent teachers. When your raised to have a curious mind, it becomes impossible to be a bigot for long.

In order to recognize the failure of ideology to bring peace on earth, one must first admit the failure of ones unquestioning faith. We must determine the difference between truth and what feels good. Faith in a divine "parent" looking over our destinies is comforting, but this hope is in no way concretely reflected in the measurable world. Actually, instead of a loving cosmic designer who has made this universe, we are indeed left with a very harsh inhuman drill sergeant that is getting the smartest and most adaptable organisms through a series of difficult survivalist trials. If we do not work together, I fear we will all lose the test.

If you find this line of thought repulsive, consider for a moment a thought experiment: You and your friends encounter a "crazy" person who is convinced there is an elephant in the room. You and your friends are equally certain that the elephant isn't there and instinctively say, "No one else sees it, it's just not there..". It is easier to see someone with an unverified opinion as a madman. But isn't it odd that, when a group is captivated by misguided beliefs, they rarely question themselves with the same scrutiny? When something is collectively agreed upon it seems more plausible. Yet, if all the data and the lessons of history show us that only through diversity and interaction every great civilization was possible, why do we cling to ancient divisive ideologies?

Science is, in a way, a form of intellectual consensus, or an ideology of sorts. The difference is, that something is not scientifically accepted until it can be proven through a repetition of an experiment. Science is held to the criteria of proving. Ideology demands faith, because it cannot be definitively proven, and conveniently has the caveat of "divine mystery", to hide behind. Our collective addiction to self-significance, and the infallibility of our conclusions that entails, is yet another challenge to overcome. The obsession with the personal ego narrative is the prehensile tail of the mind; a useless remnant of an earlier stage of evolution. I believe traditional cosmologies will suffer the same fate. Mystery and wonder is the ideal place to use science to shed light. In order to admit science offers a better model of reality one must admit not being an expert on every subject. It is through an acceptance of ones limitations, and the superior technique of scientific inquiry, that we overcome error. Reason therefore requires a loss of control over cosmic meaning. Those who fear losing control would rather watch the world burn, than accept humility for the purpose of living in peace.

(see failure to be honest)

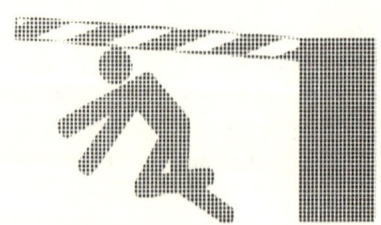

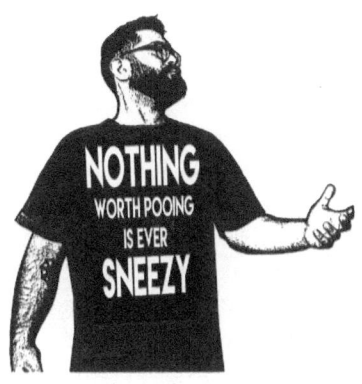

WHY DOES THIS ALWAYS HAPPEN TO ME?

Nature wants you to know you're part of a great march towards higher consciousness (or greater complexity if you dislike floral language). Nature suggests that the "project" of life on earth seems to be towards more advanced or, at the very least, more effective organism. Consider our offspring, you instinctively know that we have a duty to raise children properly. Because you know it doesn't happen on it's own, and it is careful work. Our societies can't survive without grown ups to tend to them. Ideally as you mature you become capable of taking on responsibility for your society. We often forget, that regardless of our faith or secular opinions, **we** are the ones keeping our world functioning. There is no magical force at play, it's just us "little people" making this whole civilization thing keep running. Either through our own efforts, or the complicity to a larger government. Nature is essentially the first layer of nurturing life. We are therefore required to be guardians of our world and the lives within it.

I realize it's awfully hard to stay present of mind when it feels like life is taking a steaming dump on all our plans. I also know it's really hard to have aspirations for higher consciousness when you can't pay your heating bill, or don't even have the option. But we keep fighting, all the same, in order to survive. Because we must, because nothing is going to come along and do it for us. No government, or faith, or alien, or singularity, or magic mushrooms, or technology can make you better at the art of living. We must be the adult in our own lives – no other. This is also true for child rearing: ultimately the child is learning on their own, the parent is simply facilitating. Government is an aid, not an all forgiving rich daddy. Nor should we eliminate government as we would be at the mercy of oligarchs. So a thoughtful balance must be struck.

We are trapped in this timeline of struggle because of our minds and the external contingencies of life. Fortunately, time is helpful for stringing together stories. Stories are a way to share complex information through a kind performance. Similarly, we can learn through spending time at the theater, or with a great fiction book, or a movie. Ideally, through identification, these stories save us from having to live out that narratives' struggles or "moral" individually. We can sometimes learn valuable shortcuts to life in our stories. We gain wisdom from knowing the history of governance and the fate of previous civilizations. Just as we see the unfolding of time in a fictional story and how it illustrates cause

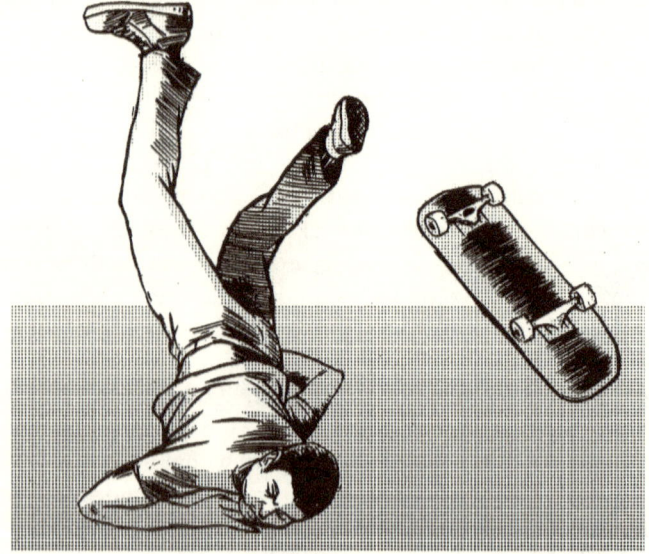

and effect, so does time "teach" us our own consequences.

In our life, we experience many stories along our path of development. We should not live in just one story forever, there are so many books to be opened. The book of first love, the book of acceptance, the book of sadness, the book of redemption, and

AN EXQUISITE FAILURE

even the book of anger to name a few. These books are all beautiful in a very particular way. We are always distracted by the story book of our lives, but we must occasionally look up from the page and remember that it is only one of many books. Ideology is a book you can read and learn from, but it is ultimately a work of fiction. The story may be an illusion but we take it very seriously. Though how else can the story give you it's treasure, if there isn't a bit of drama? Life on earth exists because of the space that "mistakes" make in an otherwise unforgiving physics. The physical laws do not function in a zero tolerance environment, and neither does wisdom. The story isn't interesting, if there isn't something at stake. In order for there to be a drama, disaster must be a possibility.

When we ask, "Why does this always happen to me?", we are really trying to present a suspicion the universe is picking on us. Appealing to some kind of celestial judge that will take mercy on our pathetic lives. Or we seek some divine purpose to our pain. In fairness to our frustration though, life presents a great deal of evidence that it **is** against us. Just to have some perspective on nature's humbling power, here's a list showing the death toll from the top recorded natural disasters:

1.	1931	1,000,000–4,000,000	China floods
2.	1887	900,000–2,000,000	Yellow River flood
3.	1556	830,000	Shaanxi earthquake
4.	1839	300,000	Indian cyclone, India

Just for comparison, here's a list of medical advances with the similar dates as above:

1.	1928	Penicillin discovered.
2.	1882	First vaccine for rabies
3.	1590	Invention of the microscope.
4.	1842	First use of ether as a general anesthetic.

Pick one of the medical discoveries above, and try to calculate how many lives you think it saved or improved. Ideology has yet to save lives, it only soothes egos. Our species keeps fighting to overcome our vulnerability to nature's onslaught. The strange thing about this relationship is: would we be as smart and capable if the universe just took it easy on us? We have developed all of our technology in order to survive this planet, and most of it because of failure to do so in the past. Clinging to old answers has garnered no benefit. Attachment to an ancient metaphysics will send you towards the dodo's fate.

While we have made steps to making earth more hospitable for us, we simultaneously seek new dangers by choice. This is very strange. For example, we explore the deepest sea, and now the cold vacuum of space. We seek to explore places even more hostile than earth, and we are continuously creating new and unforeseen environmental risks. This earth, we have tried so hard to subdue to our will, is now beginning to become even more toxic than before our populating it. Because of our devices we have become the single greatest threat to the ecosystem. So our failures and struggles are intertwined with all of our gains? Apparently the recipe for creating advanced species resembles taking one step forward and two steps back.. Maybe our struggle with religion is necessary?

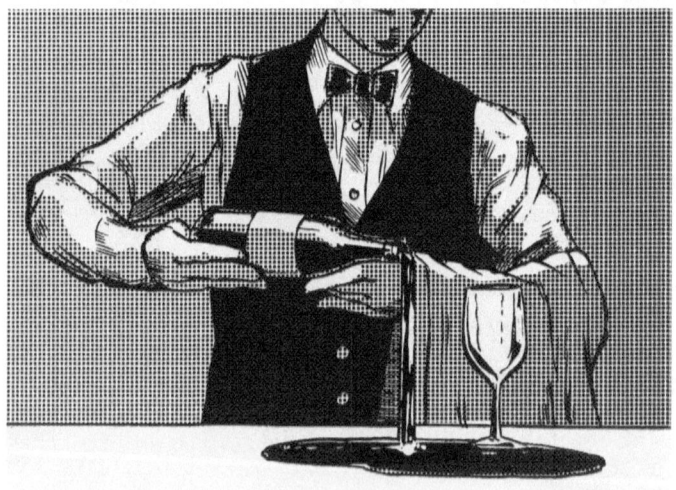

This brings me to the idea that nature already gives us a template from which to answer these questions. Evolution is not a straight line, nor is it in any way intentional in the way humans make decisions. What evolution does show us though is that when a good idea comes around and is allowed thrive, life abounds. DNA is a good metaphor for the development of life on earth. We have so much to learn from this, now not so hidden, "life code". It's as if all organisms are an algorithm in their characteristic patterns emerging from infinite probabilities. I wager in some strange way, the discovery of DNA is inseparable from humanities destiny. I do not believe that the development of advanced bio-engineering technologies, a better understanding of neurology, the development of quantum physics, and the pursuit for sustainable energy are all coinciding coincidentally. I believe that without these challenges, humanity would not have the specific and necessary pressures to advance as species. Like DNA, it's the random mutation that often creates a jump in progress. Our species seems to be moving towards a greater and greater integration with our beloved tech. Our devices are beginning to blur into our biology. Are moving towards a cybernetic epoch?

A plausible alternative outcome, is a mass extinction event. A cataclysmic decrease in human population due to infection or war. For example a global political catastrophe, due to unsustainable economic inequality. The zealot would say judgment day! But as is so often with abstract guesses about the future of humanity – the truth will often end up being out of the reach of our imaginations. My optimism that life on earth is a process towards a kind of higher consciousness is balanced by an awareness that nature occasionally does a reboot. **What difference does it make if we are doomed, shouldn't we fight for our future regardless?** Why would you accept ecological disaster as inevitable? Why would you accept a cosmic apocalypse as as absolute truth? You are being sold these narratives by others. Should you not make your own opinion before walking off a cliff with a bunch of lemmings?

(see a failure of imagination)

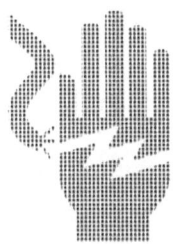

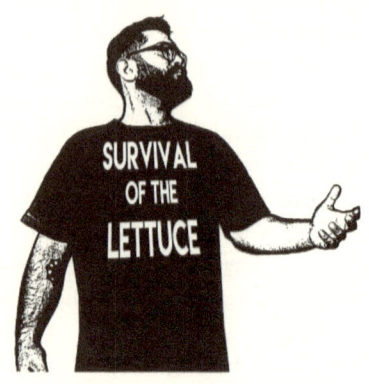

HOW TO FALL EFFECTIVELY

What is a fall? Why is falling so perennial as a metaphor for humans? Why do toddlers have to fall? So they can learn to stand up and walk, right? Try standing when your leg is severely asleep. You will soon realize how important your nervous system is! Walking upright is a particularity of our humanness. We stand, as a norm. "To stand" can be a way of being, could be a calling, or a mission in our language. "To stand firm, to take a stand, to stand upright, to stand with eyes open". These are specific human sentiments. When we stand looking outward, we see the world with greater clarity. We look out at the horizon to see what lies ahead. This is a unique dignity. Inexplicably we stand, even though physics and world are seemingly against it. The universe we find ourselves in, does not care if we survive, or vanish into nothing. The greatest fall of all is deaths. Could it be that even this finality is one from which we can arise from?

If you fell down yesterday, stand up today.

H.G. Wells

We fall and get up. Some of us locked into existential suffering, and feelings of hopeless. Some search for ghosts from before they where born. People stare into the quiet silence of the stars and wonder what it is all about, and dream up new ghosts and

AN EXQUISITE FAILURE

new rituals. We gather in groups and choose a common way of life and a common enemy. Sometimes we intoxicate ourselves and dream bizarre symbolic dreams. Our ancestors would cling to their loved ones in a dark cave, staring at a fire, hoping tomorrow will be easier. We *fall* in love, and then have our hearts broken. How could we possibly survive falling in so many ways?

How do we fall from the tower, we have built, in our own image?

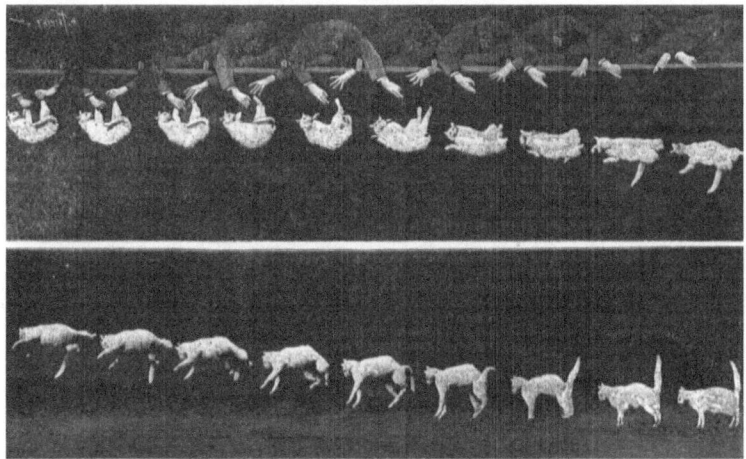

The Journal Nature, 1894

Common sense would tell us to, "go limp". We are less likely to hurt ourselves if we don't stiffen up during a fall. So it goes, for the transmogrification of the consciousness. One must let go. We must be supple and yielding. Like the young bamboo, the Kung Fu master suggests. Become so flexible that you cannot be broken. To float on water because you don't tighten up. But what does that look like, in regards to failure in life and art?

> *I am not concerned that you have fallen.. I am concerned that*
> *you arise.*
>
> *Abraham Lincoln*

I still have anxiety when confronted with strangers. I still worry if I'll mess up when I try something new. I still question every piece of art I make, until I start to hate it more than any critic could. I still haven't learned to fall gracefully every time. I still haven't learned to admit my failures thoughtfully in every moment. But when I allow myself to "float" or even just loosen my mental grip on the project at hand, **it makes itself**. Many creative or athletic people describe "being in the zone", a kind of quieted mind where the movements seem to happen on automatic. The sort of Zen space of absolute "nowness" that only spiritual folks seem to be willing to talk about. The mind that does not describe or plan. The mind that eases the grip of ego over the organism, and accepts the unknowable context. "Trusting the process", if you prefer a utilitarian interpretation.

So if you are painting, try "letting the paint tell you what it wants". In life, letting the events unfold and responding with a calm mind. Unencumbered with forcing of outcomes through control. Truly, easier said then done – this is why we fail. Failure makes you humble, and opens you to new paths only when you are open to it. "I married the wrong person". Now you know how to spot a 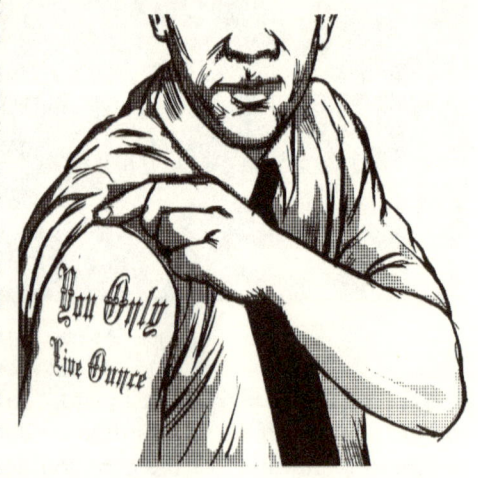 better companion. "I ruined this painting". Now you know when to stop and let the painting stew for a while. "I said something I regret". Now you know to stop, and think, before you speak.

The patience a parent has to give to a child originates from the ability to forgive their own perceived sins. If one can't see the goodness in themselves, how can we expect them (or anyone) to notice it in others? Being a "loser" can break your will, or make you the strongest person in the room. The difference is in the response to the fall, and the empathy it may instill. Controlling a child doesn't work. Children are too expansive to be contained, instead try to redirect the energy rather than contain it. **Embrace the informed free fall.**

AN EXQUISITE FAILURE

When I was in grade school. I went to the playground near my house in the projects, by myself. It's funny calling it that because, where we lived, was so manicured compared to government housing on the East Coast. When suddenly, I flew to the ground and scrapped my chin. I turned around and realized a bigger kid had pushed me. My head still spinning, I stood up and tried to say something like, "why are you doing this"? He shoved me down again, I don't know why but I got up again instinctively. This happened over and over. He kept mocking my questions, and telling me to **"stay down"**. I realize, looking back, it was good that he didn't have the courage to punch or kick me, because that would have been much worse. Finally, I just sat there looking at him, not understanding why he was doing this. He left finally. I don't know what happen after that because I don't recall seeing him again. I can imagine though. The parents in the neighborhood where 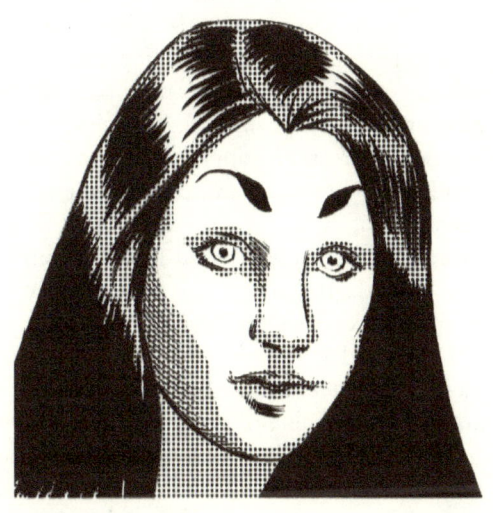 always keeping track of the "goings on", due to the various risks. His father probably beat the crap out of him. Maybe that sort of thing happened often to him, and maybe that's where all his random rage was coming from. It must have been terrifying to have a father that makes you feel powerless and afraid. Then again, maybe I deserved that boys rage, for some reason? I guess feeling empathy for that angry little boy is my attempt to stand back up one last time to the bully. That experience changed me forever. I had experienced a random act of violence, and I chose to never allow myself to do that to another person. I would like you, as well, to see that even trauma, humiliation, and suffering can be a deep well of inspiration for great art. Or, a strategy for what I believe is a healthier perspective.

I would like to highlight the American educational system and it's failure, as a culprit for the unhealthy relationship with failure many have us have been indoctrinated in. I would like to utilize the flaws, as the very data, from which a better method can emerge. The basic premise of the American can-do-attitude is based on the idea: if you work hard and do well at your studies/job, you will be rewarded. The technique of choice, is rote order following and repetition of information. This is represented through standardized testing, and a reward/punishment system that is used in the classroom and then carries on into the workforce. This method is great for factory workers. It is ideal for jobs that utilized semi-skilled labor. Now that manufacturing has left the US, there is increasingly higher demand for creativity and abstract problem solving skills. As we see that our educational ideology is not adaptive we must ask ourselves what characteristics may have the opposite effect? It appears imagination and creativity are not produced by routine, and training for tests. We must question the premises of what we currently think is a logical meritocracy. Is institutionalized merit, loyal followers, and mindless elbow grease, the ingredients of a sharp leader with adaptive solutions? Furthermore, does the high tech industry need more "drones" or, does it need minds that can imagine solutions for problems we have never encountered before? Could this apply to statesmanship, and the maintaining of our systems of survival?

The most disastrous American belief is that wealth is a reflection of individual worth. Can you actually justify that an heir to a fortune, who makes their money through inheritance and investments, is contributing to society in the same way a teacher or a physicist does? It is is patently absurd. Why? Let us consider the current state of global capital that has worked against the benefit of most people and profited a small minority on an unprecedented scale. This system of currency that exists in a world of speculation and abstract values, has become inaccessible to the largest portion of humanity. We are to believe that stock value is a reflection of the of a business' probability of success. A system that no longer has a basis in physical reality, yet is used to determine real outcomes. It is based on a faith in a system, and protected by the largest military in the history of the world. Anything based on faith is open to manipulation and delusions. Let us consider the numerous crimes crimes of corporations in light of our naive belief that wealth

AN EXQUISITE FAILURE

instills special virtue. Let's not forget the housing bubble, the games that where played with people's pensions and savings. Blind faith in any system will leave you a patsy. I don't need to argue this idea, the failure is obvious. I don't think anyone actually believes our economic system is fair and balanced. I think instead, the powerful cling to the hope that they can squeeze in some unearned profit for ourselves, before the whole thing comes crashing down.

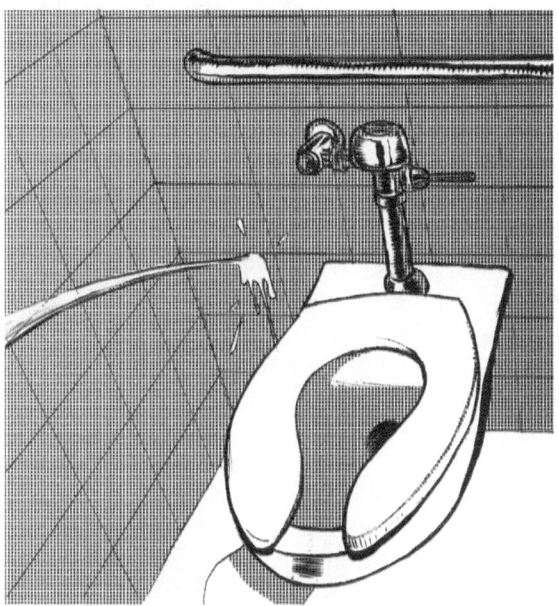

Having shiny stuff is no reflection on your merit as a person, and having theoretical money is even more elusive. It begs the question, why do people follow an agenda which, time and time again, hurts their own interests and clearly doesn't work? When has blindly trusting the powerful with our destinies ever worked out in favor of the common man? Every other "isim" has failed. Yet, as a herd we keep getting duped over and over, Why? I think, because we don't know how to accept our nation's failings as ultimately our own failure. Because trudging through the slow deliberate work of building a functioning society, is less sexy than charging ahead with mindless greedy confidence.

Falling gracefully requires humility, generosity, and honesty. In regards to economic progress, it is very difficult to stop a corrupted system by using the system itself. Sorry, but **centrism in an insane asylum is just choosing the least psychotic option**. One must be courageous, ingenious, and have a very cohesive community to solve problems of this magnitude. These qualities are difficult to nurture in our celebrity obsessed distraction reality. How are we supposed to be thoughtful, when our senses are barraged with silicon filled, artificial controversy producing, narcissistic "person products"? Educating our children in how to pass tests within a bankrupt system is not a life skill they need. Democracy and it's success comes from a thousand little mistakes and improvements, not from standing firm in ones failure. I suggest we move away from the oversimplified "Make America Great Again!" sentiment. Instead, a careful process of identifying needs and addressing the successes and failures of previous attempts. **If people continue to want simple answers to complex problems, all they will ever get is a con man with an idiotic slogan.**

The most obvious place to look for answers on how to improve a situation, that isn't getting better, is ask yourself what has been the same for too long? Returning to the same old slogans and mentalities clearly will not garner new or better results. The US in the 1950's was based on countless unaddressed lies, and the economic success was temporary and artificial. The romanticism regarding this time is simply veiled racism.

(see the failure of materialism)

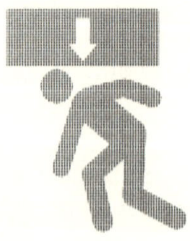

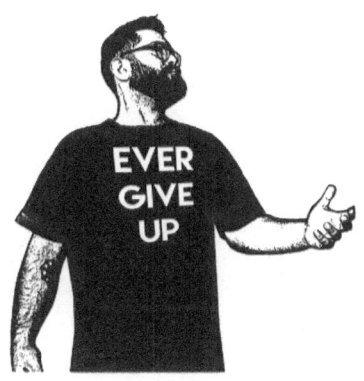

THE WRONG NUMBERS

There are more than 200 classified forms of mental illness. There is no agreed upon definition of sanity. There are an estimated 30,000 human diseases known to medicine. There is roughly 13 million doctors on earth and the World Health Organization estimates a 2.3 million shortfall from what is needed globally. **In 3,400 years, humans have experienced peace for 268** of those years. Roughly 108 billion have been born onto this earth, of them 870 of them have received Nobel prizes. In 6000 years of human civilization, we have yet to adequately explain the nature of our existence, in a satisfactory way to 46% of the worlds population. 77% of Americans believe in angels. Only 40% percent will accept climate change is a reality. Only 25% of Americans believe the Earth revolves around the sun. On average the human body contains ten times more bacterial cells than human cells. There are more things living on your skin than there are people living on the planet. It's not actually bad to pick up baby birds and return them to their nests. Our blood has never been blue, in or outside, of your body. There are not different parts of the tongue for different tastes. The Milky Way contains somewhere in the area of 100,000,000,000 Earth-like planets. Chameleons don't actually change their color to blend in with the environment.

All men make mistakes, but a good man yields when he knows his course is wrong, and repairs the evil. The only crime is pride.

Sophocles, Antigone

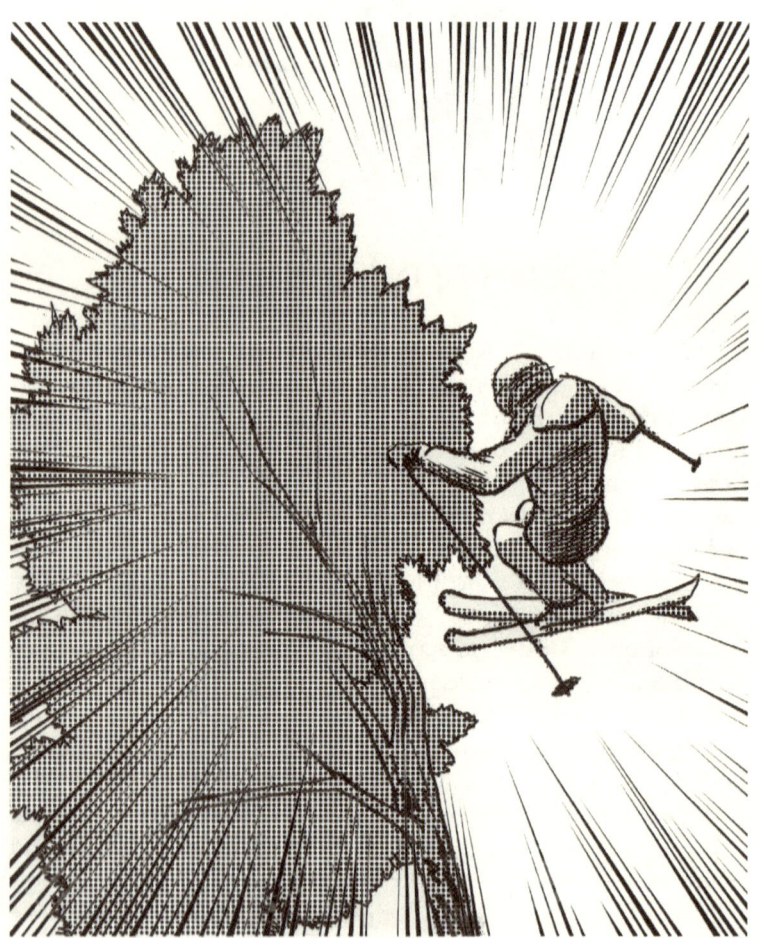

Most of us operate under a collection of opinions that are rarely questioned. Our perceptions are often inherited and we often suffer from a kind of conceptual Phenomenalism[3]. We don't

---

3   Phenomenalism infers that physical objects cannot be proven to exist in themselves, but only as perceptions or sense experiences alone.

seem to believe our instincts and would rather leave things "officially explained". Most folks don't ponder "meaning of life questions" unless a situation arises to force them to do so. Such as funerals or births. Take a moment to think about the ideas you take for granted, and then imagine, what if truth was the exact opposite of what you thought? How would you process this? How would you deal with the embarrassing realization you'd been walking around blind to your own existence? More difficultly, how would your friends and family deal with this change? When we transform, it often requires a sudden revelation regarding something that would normally be invisible to us. Artists have to think this way all the time, and that's why the common myth about us is that we are crazy.

> *Science, my lad, is made up of mistakes, but they are mistakes which it is useful to make, because they lead little by little to the truth.*
>
> *Jules Verne, A Journey to the Center of the Earth*

For example, is your body a vehicle for your brain, or is your brain just another organ in a body? In other words, your "mind" and feelings of being an individual consciousness, are in fact a byproduct of a sense organ. Like bile from the spleen. Is your brain a giant nerve feeling the environment to keep the body alive? Could it be that the body, in other words is the real you, and your mind is a fiction? To be clinically accurate, we are a DNA vehicle. Furthermore, like the very first single cell organisms that emerged from RNA replicators that organized into patterns, your body is a product of the ingredients that where randomly available in the primordial soup. We could have just as easily been silicon based organisms. Your body is inseparable from the ecosystem it inhabits. The human mind gives the illusion of separation from the environment because it is a more convenient way to identify nutrients and dangers. You are not a passenger **in** your organism, "you" are a phantom. A ghost made by a completely integrated "Goldilocks" planet housed in a DNA transit system. The ghost in the shell, is just more shell.

(see a failure to detach)

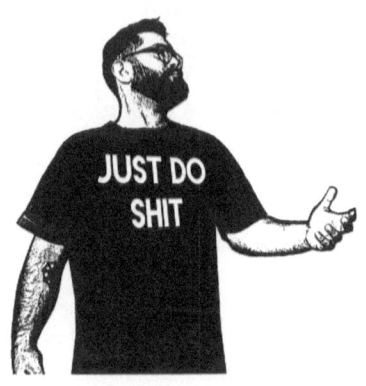

MAKING BAD DRAWINGS

Making bad drawings is the surest way to make good drawings. Now of course, not everyone agrees what is a good drawing, but bad drawings seem to stand out to a wider group of people. Some drawings are so bad they are good. Some drawings are so well done that they are terrible – like an overcooked steak. Further still are those difficult drawings that are both good and bad at the same time – like an emotionally upsetting and ugly image, that is so powerful and revelatory, you are haunted by it.

Sometimes you draw a picture in your head that's so real it could eat your whole heart up. The pictures we draw in our heads, make us do crazy things. The drawing of fear, paranoia, or the picture of abject loss can consume our souls. What if the ultimate failure in drawing was to believe that failure is a thing that can even happen in drawings? What if **there is no failure but only layers of information?** One after the other, like waves crashing against the shore of your being, insights come from the drawing. What if screwing up, is the only way to draw properly? Metaphors tend to be weak explanations for the human condition. But drawings can cover a lot of territory very quickly, and have a way of not being restricted by grammar.

Consider for a moment that drawing is a language that can often transcend cultural differences, and sometimes compel discovering new perspectives. Drawings have been used to describe the design of a building, the movement of the stars, and romantic love. Drawings are equally good at expressing ideas, feelings, observations, and sometimes even things that are impossible to describe otherwise. Furthermore, a drawings ability to present us with contradictions in a way that is plausible, is nothing short of amazing. It takes many words to describe a Möbius strip, while a single drawing can explain it's qualities nearly instantaneously.

Let us now consider drawings relation to failure. How do drawings fail? What advantage is there for utilizing the knowledge gained from failure?

> *I forgive all living beings,*
> *may all living beings forgive me.*
> *All in this world are my friends,*
> *I have no enemies.*
>
> *Jain prayer*

I forgive all my bad drawings, may all my sketches "forgive" me. All my drawings are my friends, I have no bad drawings. If we begin to use drawing as a learning process rather than a method for producing a product, it opens the range of possibilities of what a "drawing" could be. Furthermore, if the ambition is learning, the results will vary as widely as your willingness to explore. In other words, the more open you are to seeking new information, the better your drawings get. Or, at the very least, more diverse and interesting.

Therefore drawings cannot fail, **ever**. The advantage of this perspective is that every drawing becomes material from which you can increasingly improve upon the following drawings. Artistic practice becomes a nesting doll that becomes more and more wondrous as it grows. Not moving towards perfection, but instead becoming more complex and/or various. For example, I prefer the aesthetic of a rainforest and all it's vibrance to the barren surface of mars. But I can also see there is beauty in that stark rugged landscape as well. Just as there is something to admire in a simpler way of life. But it is in the great array of options that we discern the beautiful characteristics of each. For example, flavors in food are all understood by comparison. How would you know what tastes spicy, if all you eat is white bread every day? If you listen to only one genre of music, how would you really know if it's your favorite? Many people think they don't like something, but simply haven't given it a chance. It is in the option to sample from real life, rather than our prejudices, where learning and growth occurs. This is why censorship and bigotry are terrible cancers on human development. We must never stifle a person, even if we find their ideas repulsive. You should always try the dish before deciding you don't enjoy the taste. We must try to give all of the varieties of life a space to exist. We must give every drawing a chance to speak to us.

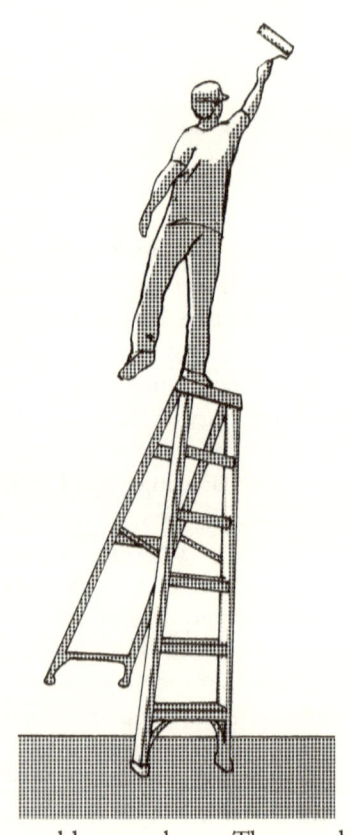

I offer the example of the earth worm. The worm is disgusting slimy, and unremarkable. It is generally not desirable to anyone but fisherman. They are not aesthetically pleasing, they don't make very good conversationalists, and are certainly are not very good pets. The worm appears to have no redeeming qualities on the surface. We don't like them, but reptiles, birds, mammals, amphibians and fish eat worms. The attraction is a matter of taste. Also the earth in which we grow our food, would most likely become useless without them. I think it's safe to say you stand more to gain by getting to know a person, you might not initially like, than trying to have a relationship with a worm. Also, a person could have so many hidden talents that an earthworm, as useful as they are, could never have. They could become your best friend! Earthworms are not such great conversationalists.

When we make a bad drawing in our head of a person we don't like, and never try to draw them again, we do ourselves a

AN EXQUISITE FAILURE

great disservice. We limit the possibilities of our own lives because we choose to believe the first attempt at drawing our mental portrait was the final word. But how can this be, when all things are changing, always? Why would you ever believe the first drawing you ever did was the best that is possible? Even Leonardo revised his paintings countless times? Drawing is the process of rehearsing, and presenting the final play simultaneously. Finished – incomplete – ongoing. Like the very flow of the Tao.

(see a failure of technique)

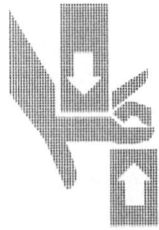

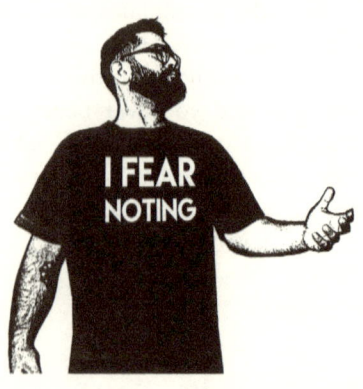

FAILURE TO FINISH

    This is a failure to make a cohesive statement. The book of failure is not complete without totally botching the wrap up. Abandoning all it's thoughts and examples in a manner that is unconvincing and utterly lacking any endearing final thoughts. Ideally this is where the juicy mind-blowing one-liners should be. Going to drop that ball on that.. Yup, here's where my literary treasure should crescendo into a choir. While I'm raised to the heavens by a blinding white light that's caressing my now (inexplicably) ripped abs. My flowing (equally unexplained) blonde mane begins to form a golden halo around my visage, and I say unto you the Loser's Prayer:

> *Behold, I have failed at everything I've ever tried. I am the C- and F, I am the fart during the funeral, take shelter in my self-inflicted wedgie! For ours is the leftover shrunken meatloaf, and the diarrhea that follows.. you are my clod and the staph, in the name of the bother, and the skunk, and the oily roast. Amen*

    No instead, I will offer some closing thoughts on my conceptual train wreck. When I attempted to organize my thoughts on the nature of failure, I couldn't pin down the specific ingredient that it offered. I found that the main element in my experiences of failure was memory. Memories of the events, my thoughts on what I should have done, and the awkward feelings it inspired. It seemed that failure has a kind of "area effect"; something that has a generalized cloud of qualities instead of a concrete form. It was too boring to point at, "an event that did not meet satisfactory expectations" as an honest description of failure. We all know that it is so much more emotional and complex then that. I began to write this book from the perspective I was advocating, the best way to learn is by trying. As we make mistakes and false steps, we begin to see a better way. So here's my "better way":

There are two major constants in human emotional life, disappointment and a desire to be successful. We are obviously too biased in favor of the desired outcome of winning. We cannot passively accept the consistent repetition of ruined hopes, and failed dreams, it is just too much to ask. Therefore, if we should change our interpretation of **failure into rehearsal**, so then it ceases to be an error. Now the "screw up" instead becomes practice for the win. Failure becomes the material from which we a build a successful life. The alternative is depressing, and ultimately no more objective. If you see every failure as a necessary step towards a better life, then the world is on your side and everyone is your friend.

To be an artist is to fail, as no other dare to fail, that is his world..
Samuel Beckett

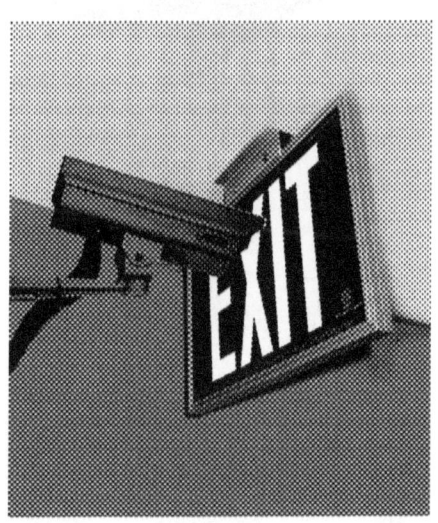

ABOUT THE AUTHOR

Reza Ghanad is an artist, art handler, and writer. He resides in Philadelphia with his wife and cats.

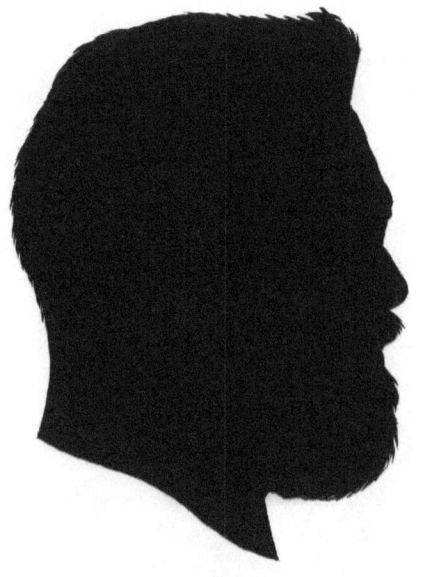

screamingdodopress.com

instagram.com/rezaghanadart/

www.ingramcontent.com/pod-product-compliance
Lightning Source LLC
Chambersburg PA
CBHW030509220526
45464CB00006B/2725